Comprehension Mini-Lessons

Main Idea & Summarizing

by LeAnn Nickelsen
with Sarah Glasscock

D1275504

NEW YORK • TORONTO • LONDON • AUCKLAND • SYDNEY
MEXICO CITY • NEW DELHI • HONG KONG • BUENOS AIRES

SCHOLASTIC
Teaching
Resources

I would like to thank the following people for this book:

my husband, Joel, and my twin children, Keaton and Aubrey, for encouraging and supporting me with the goal of writing this book.

my parents, Jim and Dolores Heim, for helping me with ideas and for all their support. Thanks Mom and Dad for creating the "Who Am I?" activity.

Virginia Dooley, my senior editor, for helping me become a more concise writer and for all of the writing opportunities she has given me.

Sarah Glasscock, my cowriter, and Sarah Longhi, my editor, who spent numerous hours checking over this book to make sure it was perfect.

my sister, Sherry DeVilbiss, for being a great, supportive friend. I know you really wanted your name to be in a book, so here it is (hahaha).

my education friends who have taught with me through the years. You know so much and have contributed so much time and effort. You know who you are!

Grapevine-Colleyville ISD in Texas for supplying me with resources and advice. Anne Simpson, your knowledge is valued by many. Thanks for the help with summarization and main idea.

Mary Howard, a friend, educator, and professional developer, for her ideas on main idea and summarization—"Rip and Tear" and "quick writes."

Jim Baumann for providing the inspiration for the table graphic organizer.

The PROVE It strategy on pages 47–49 was adapted from: Prove It: Whole Language Strategies for Secondary Students by M. Bixby (Richard Owen Publishing, 1988).

—LeAnn Nickelsen

Cover design by Norma Ortiz
Cover art by Jason Robinson
Interior design by Sydney Wright
Interior illustrations by Teresa Southwell
Page 46 pencil illustration by Milk & Cookies

Copyright© 2004 by LeAnn Nickelsen and Sarah Glasscock. All rights reserved.
ISBN 0-439-43835-7
Printed in the U.S.A.

9 10   40   09 08

Contents

Introduction

The *Comprehension Mini-Lessons* Series

National and state standards, and schools across the country require all students to master a set of reading objectives, with an emphasis on these key comprehension areas: main idea, summarizing, inference, cause and effect, point of view, fact and opinion, sequencing, and context clues. For me and the teachers I work with, teaching students to deepen their comprehension has always required several creative lessons for each reading objective to ensure that everyone achieves success. Customizing each lesson plan is a lot of work, and that's where this series of high-interest mini-lessons—the product of years of classroom lesson successes—comes to the rescue.

Each book in this series provides you with several different mini-lessons for each objective, which appeal to different learning styles and help you reach each and every learner. The mini-lessons include activities and real-world examples, so that students have fun learning the reading objective and find the skills they learn useful in their everyday reading and pertinent to their lives.

About This Book

This book presents lessons that teach students skills and strategies for understanding main idea and summarizing.

Main Idea

When readers synthesize the main idea of a text, they capture a big picture of what the whole passage is about. Articulating this big picture helps readers summarize what they've read, call on the important details that support the main idea, weed out superfluous details, and introduce a main idea backed up by supporting details in their own writing.

Summarizing

Summarizing, or being able to recount the key events or steps in a text, enables the brain to process this newly learned information and link ideas in a sequence. Developing skills in summarizing helps save readers time and energy; by creating an outline or a shortened version of the text, they can keep track of important information in a sequence without getting bogged down by details. Summarizing is a valuable real-life skill used in many situations, from social settings, where friends might share book recommendations by offering plot summaries, to work settings, where project summaries are often required in reports to supervisors.

How to Use This Book

You'll find six mini-lessons on main idea and five mini-lessons on summarizing, with activities that stimulate different learning styles (visual, auditory, and kinesthetic). I

recommend teaching the lessons sequentially. The first lesson introduces the objective in simple terms. The subsequent lessons elaborate on the objective and offer students different skills to better understand it. The last lesson features the objective in a test-taking format, which helps familiarize students with the test language and structure. A final project pulls the whole concept together and offers students an opportunity to demonstrate creatively what they learned in the mini-lessons. They also get to share their learning with other classmates when they complete a project. Whenever students teach other students what they have learned, the learning becomes more cemented in their brains.

Notice that each lesson contains anticipatory sets, which enable you to grab students' attention when you open the lesson, and special closures to end the lesson, so that students' brains can have another opportunity to absorb the learning. Also included are activities that you can send home to extend the learning in another real-world setting.

I suggest beginning your instruction with the main idea mini-lessons and then teaching the summarizing mini-lessons. By introducing the main idea objectives first, students are prepared to summarize: They can differentiate between the main idea and supporting sentences, identify relevant and irrelevant information, and find the main idea of several paragraphs within a passage. These skills help them write focused, concise summaries of both short and long pieces of writing.

—LeAnn Nickelsen

Young Adult Fiction Resources

In addition to the excerpts from literature that you'll find in the lessons, here are some additional suggestions for literature that supports the objectives in this book (NOTE: Picture books like those listed in the summarizing section provide short, vivid stories with memorable events that support summary writing for upper-grade students.)

Books That Support Developing a Main Idea

Fritz, Jean. *And Then What Happened, Paul Revere?* New York: Scholastic, 1988.

Pène du Bois, William. *The 21 Balloons.* New York: Viking Press, 1947.

Lowry, Lois. *Number the Stars.* New York: Dell Publishing, 1989.

Spinelli, Jerry. *Stargirl.* New York: Random House, 2000.

Books That Support Summarizing

Aliki. *A Weed is a Flower: The Life of George Washington Carver.* New Jersey: Prentice Hall, 1965.

Lionni, Leo. *Swimmy.* New York: Knopf, 1992. (picture book)

Burton, Virginia Lee. *The Little House.* Boston: Houghton Mifflin, 1978. (picture book)

Maclachlan, Patricia. *Sarah, Plain and Tall.* New York: Harper Junior Books, 1987.

Main Idea

Main Idea: The Big Picture

Opening the Lesson

❋ Write one main idea sentence and two detail sentences on three sentence strips. (NOTE: You might want to refer to the main idea as the topic sentence of a paragraph.)

❋ I begin this lesson by thinking aloud about how the main idea and details relate to each other. For instance, I might say, *The main idea is the big picture of an event. It lets the reader know what a paragraph or passage is about. The main idea is a general statement about the topic or subject. Details are specific statements about the same topic. They describe and support the main idea.*

❋ Then I display the three sentence strips. I explain that one of the sentences is the main idea and the other two sentences are details that support it. This activity offers a good opportunity for students to work together, so I ask pairs to discuss which sentence is the main idea and which are the details and then to share their conclusions with the rest of the class.

❋ Now that my students have a concrete example of a main idea and details, I create another set of sentences that relate to a theme or topic that we're studying. I model the differences between main idea and details until I'm sure my students understand the concept.

Teaching the Lesson

1. Have partners discuss how main ideas and details help structure a paragraph. Solicit ideas from students and synthesize a definition that can serve as a model for the class. For example, you might say, *A paragraph is made up of sentences that are about the same subject or topic. The main idea is what a paragraph is mostly about. Details are the sentences that describe and support the main idea of a paragraph. The main idea and its details appear in the same paragraph.* Write the class main idea explanation on chart paper and hang it so that students can refer to it throughout your unit.

2. Display the transparency of The Big Picture that you made, and provide the following visual memory clue: *Think of the main idea*

Objective

Students distinguish between main idea and details.

Materials

6 sentences strips, marker, magazines, classroom objects

Reproducibles

The Big Picture, page 9 (Make 1 double-sided copy for each student. Make 1 transparency.)

Main Idea vs. Details, page 10 (Make 1 copy for each student.)

Tip

Ask students how they learned about main idea and details last year. You may be able to build upon vocabulary and examples that are familiar to them..

7

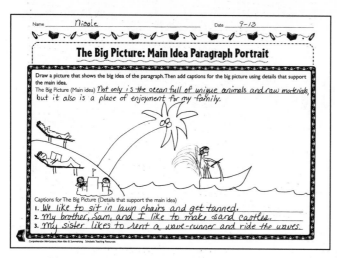

Name ___Nicole___   Date ___9-13___

The Big Picture: Main Idea Paragraph Portrait

Draw a picture that shows the big idea of the paragraph. Then add captions for the big picture using details that support the main idea.

The Big Picture (Main idea) _Not only is the ocean full of unique animals and raw materials, but it also is a place of enjoyment for my family._

Captions for The Big Picture (Details that support the main idea)
1. _We like to sit in lawn chairs and get tanned._
2. _My brother, Sam, and I like to make sand castles._
3. _My sister likes to rent a wave-runner and ride the waves._

Comprehensive Mini-Lessons: Main Idea & Summarizing Scholastic Teaching Resources

as the big picture. The details are the caption to the big picture. Ask students to help you complete it. I usually call on a volunteer to suggest a topic. Then I ask another volunteer to think of a main idea sentence about that topic, which I write in the top box of the transparency. I continue by having students supply three detail statements about the main idea, which I enter in the caption section.

3. Now students get to complete their own big pictures. Distribute the Big Picture reproducible to each student. Have partners create their own big picture sentences and caption details. Encourage them to include an illustration. (Each partner should complete his or her own copy of the reproducible.) To stimulate their thinking about topics, I set out magazine pictures, classroom objects, or other items. Set aside class time so partners can present their completed big pictures.

4. Students can use the other side of the Big Picture reproducible for individual practice. They may choose their own topics, or you may suggest several.

Closing the Lesson

Use one or more of these activities to wrap up the mini-lesson.

❋ **Auditory:** Ask students to share their individual Big Picture main ideas and details. Use the reproducible to work individually with students who are having trouble distinguishing between main ideas and details.

❋ **Journal:** Have students write a paragraph about a favorite activity or sport. The paragraph should include a main idea and at least three supporting detail sentences.

❋ **Assessment:** Use the Main Idea vs. Details reproducible to determine how well students have mastered the concept.

Answers

Main Idea vs. Details, page 10:

1. Main idea: Native American tribes lived in a variety of different dwellings.
Details: The Plains Indians used tepees that were easy to put up and take down. The Iroquois built longhouses, which were large rectangular homes. The Navaho constructed an earth-covered log dwelling called a hogan.

2. Main idea: Volcanoes can be classified by the amount of activity they produce.
Details: If a volcano has not erupted within historic times, it is inactive. An extinct volcano will probably not erupt in the future. Dormant volcanoes have been known to erupt in historic times and will probably erupt again in the future.

3. Topic sentence: I love reading, both in and out of school. (Answers may vary.)

The Big Picture: Main Idea Paragraph Portrait

Draw a picture that shows the big idea of the paragraph. Then add captions for the big picture using details that support the main idea.

The Big Picture (main idea) _____

Captions for The Big Picture (details that support the main idea)

1. _____

2. _____

3. _____

Main Idea vs. Details

In each set, write an *M* for the main idea and a *D* for detail sentences.

1.

_____ Native American tribes lived in a variety of different dwellings.

_____ The Plains Indians used tepees that were easy to put up and take down.

_____ The Iroquois built longhouses, which were large rectangular homes.

_____ The Navaho constructed an earth-covered log dwelling called a hogan.

2.

_____ If a volcano has not erupted within historic times, it is inactive.

_____ Volcanoes can be classified by the amount of activity they produce.

_____ An extinct volcano will probably not erupt in the future.

_____ Dormant volcanoes have been known to erupt in historic times and will probably erupt again in the future.

Read the detail sentences below. Can you think of a topic sentence that states the main idea?

3. I was elected librarian for the class library. I write a book review column for our school paper. At home, I like to find a quiet space to read in my spare time. I'm usually finishing up a book that I'm going to discuss with my book club.

Topic sentence: _____

_____

Comprehension Mini-Lessons: Main Idea & Summarizing Scholastic Teaching Resources

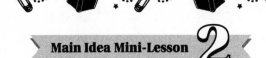

Supporting the Main Idea

Opening the Lesson

✿ This mini-lesson compares main idea and details to a table, so I ask pairs of students to think about their desks or tables. To guide them in focusing on the construction of the furniture, I say, *What keeps your table (or desk) from wobbling or falling down? What would happen if you removed one or more of the legs?*

✿ After the discussion, I tell my students that I'm going to show them how the details in a paragraph are like the legs that support a tabletop or desktop.

Teaching the Lesson

1. After distributing the Christopher Columbus and the Main Idea reproducible to students, display the Main Idea on the Table graphic organizer transparency on the overhead. Model how to record information on the graphic organizer by using the first paragraph about Columbus. (NOTE: The main idea in Paragraph 1 appears in the second sentence. This is a great example for students to see. It's important for them to realize that the first sentence of a paragraph is *not* always the topic sentence/ main idea.)

2. Ask students which sentence from the first paragraph belongs at the top of the Main Idea on the Table graphic organizer. Then have them identify which sentences are the details. Record their responses in the appropriate sections. You may find that you need to add more legs to the table or that you may not need all four legs.

3. Pass out the table graphic organizer reproducible to your students, and have them graph the second paragraph about Columbus on their own. Remind students that the main idea sentence often appears at the beginning of a paragraph, but that this isn't always the case. If some of students haven't mastered the concept, continue practicing with this graphic organizer.

Objective

Students use a graphic organizer to show how detail sentences support the main idea of a paragraph.

Reproducibles

Christopher Columbus and the Main Idea, page 13 (Make 1 copy for each student.)

Main Idea on the Table, page 14 (Make 1 transparency and 1 double-sided copy for each student.)

Tip

Remind students about the big pictures they created in Mini-Lesson 1. Encourage them to compare their big picture visuals to the Table graphic organizer.

11

Closing the Lesson

Use one or more of these activities to wrap up the mini-lesson.

✱ **Journal:** Ask students to explain how a paragraph is like a table. (This is a good time to review the definition of a simile!) What other object(s) can they think of to compare to a paragraph?

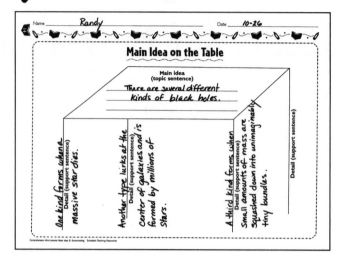

Name _____ Randy _____ Date _____ 10-26 _____

Main Idea on the Table

Main idea
(topic sentence)
There are several different kinds of black holes.

One kind forms when massive stars die.
Detail (support sentence)

Another type lurks at the center of galaxies and is formed by millions of stars.
Detail (support sentence)

A third kind forms when small amounts of mass are squashed down into unimaginably tiny bundles.
Detail (support sentence)

Detail (support sentence)

Comprehension Mini-Lessons: Main Idea & Summarizing   Scholastic Teaching Resources

✱ **Group Name:** Groups of five students can create human models of the Table graphic organizer. Write each of the following five sentences on an index card:

In their pens, the pigs squeal loudly.

The farm is a wonderful place to learn about a variety of animals.

Dogs herd the sheep across the field.

The horses gallop across the pasture.

The farmer must know about animals in order to keep them healthy.

Give an index card to each group member. They should determine who has the main idea. That student lies on the floor to represent a tabletop. The students who possess cards with supporting detail sentences become legs by lying on the floor with their heads perpendicular to and "supporting" the tabletop.

✱ **Assessment:** After students draw a Table graphic organizer on a sheet of paper, have them graph a paragraph from one of their textbooks.

Answers

Christopher Columbus and the Main Idea, page 13: (Paragraph 1) Main Idea: During these voyages, he improved his sailing skills. Details: At 15, Christopher Columbus left home to work on trading ships sailing back and forth on the Mediterranean Sea. He learned how to navigate by studying the height of the North Star at night and the position of the sun at noon. He learned how to use a compass. He could also tell where he was by watching birds, fish, driftwood, seaweed, and the color of the water. The sea had much to teach him.

(Paragraph 2) Main Idea: While the Spaniards thought the inhabitants of San Salvador were strange, it is hard to imagine how weird Columbus and his men appeared to the natives. Details: They had never seen white men before and thought perhaps they were gods or birds from the sky. The natives touched the Spaniards' beards and hands and seemed amazed that they covered their bodies. They felt Columbus's clothing and ran their hands along the edges of his sword. Columbus even gave them little bells and necklaces of glass beads in order to share their unique treasures from Spain.

Christopher Columbus and the Main Idea

Graph the sentences in each paragraph on the table graphic organizer. Write the main idea (topic sentence) on the tabletop and the details on the table legs. You can add more legs to the table. Remember—the more details there are, the sturdier the paragraph is!

Paragraph 1

At 15, Christopher Columbus left home to work on trading ships sailing back and forth on the Mediterranean Sea. During these voyages, he improved his sailing skills. Columbus learned how to navigate by studying the height of the North Star at night and the position of the sun at noon. He learned how to use a compass. By watching birds, fish, driftwood, seaweed, and the color of the water, Columbus could also tell where he was. The sea had much to teach him.

Paragraph 2

While the Spaniards thought the inhabitants of San Salvador were strange, it is hard to imagine how weird Columbus and his men appeared to the native people. They had never seen white men before and thought perhaps they were gods or birds from the sky. The natives touched the Spaniards' beards and hands and seemed amazed that they covered their bodies. They felt Columbus's clothing and ran their hands along the edges of his sword. Columbus even gave them little bells and necklaces of glass beads in order to share their unique treasures from Spain.

Main Idea on the Table

**Main Idea
(topic sentence)**

Detail (support sentence)

Detail (support sentence)

Detail (support sentence)

Detail (support sentence)

Comprehension Mini-Lessons: Main Idea & Summarizing Scholastic Teaching Resources

Which Details Are Important?

Opening the Lesson

✸ To introduce this lesson, I fill a plastic bag with a variety of differently wrapped candies (tiny candy bars, hard candy, lollipops, and so on). Then I add two objects that are unrelated to candy or to each other, for example, a pretzel and an ad for candy. This always captures my students' attention!

✸ After giving my students a chance to study the contents of the bag, I ask them to identify which items don't belong in the bag and to justify their reasoning.

✸ Then I think aloud about how a paragraph resembles the plastic bag. I usually say something like this: *The main idea of the bag is candy you can eat, and the details are the specific types of candy. Inside the bag, however, there are some objects that don't belong— food that is not a piece of candy and an advertisement for candy. The same thing can happen in a paragraph. It may contain irrelevant, or unrelated, details that seem related but do not directly support the main idea of the paragraph. They may be about the topic, but they do not support the main idea.*

Teaching the Lesson

1. The process of identifying and eliminating irrelevant details can help students highlight the key points in any text. Define and discuss the words *relevant* and *irrelevant* as necessary.

2. Place the Irrelevant Details transparency on the overhead, and read aloud the first example. Point out that there are many detail sentences, but some of these sentences don't relate well to the main idea. Although the sentences are about the topic, they don't support the main idea or "big picture."

3. Model how you found one of the irrelevant details in the paragraph. Here is what I say to my students: *I think the sentence* Other civil rights leaders worked on boycotts in southern cities, too *is an irrelevant detail. It gets away from the main idea about why Dr. King led this particular bus boycott in Montgomery.*

Objective

Students identify relevant and irrelevant details in a paragraph.

Materials

plastic bag, variety of candy, pretzel, ad for candy, paper and pens

Reproducibles

Irrelevant Details, page 17 (Make 1 transparency.)

Paragraph Rip & Tear, page 18 (Make 1 copy for each group.)

4. Go on to the second paragraph. Ask students to write on a sheet of paper the two sentences that aren't relevant details.

5. Then tell students that they get to physically rip the irrelevant details out of the third paragraph! After you read aloud the paragraph, have them

write the main idea on the Paragraph Rip & Tear reproducible. Then they should identify five to seven details, both relevant and irrelevant, from the paragraph and write them inside the detail columns.

6. Direct students to eliminate the irrelevant details by tearing or cutting off those strips. Have them explain to partners which sentences they ripped off and why. After partners have completed this task, bring all students together to compare the detail strips that are left on their pages and discuss which details they eliminated. Remind students to justify their choices.

Closing the Lesson

Use one or more of these activities to wrap up the mini-lesson.

✸ **Auditory:** Ask partners to explain to one another what they learned about details through the Rip & Tear activity. Then invite a few students to share their thoughts with the whole class. You can build on their comments.

✸ **Students Working Together:** Have each student write a paragraph about an average day at school. Their paragraphs should contain relevant and irrelevant details. Then they can exchange paragraphs with partners and use pencils to cross out the irrelevant details.

Answers

Irrelevant Details, page 17
Example 1:
Other civil rights leaders worked on boycotts in southern cities, too.
The bus was not very large.
Example 2:
These machines were greatly needed.
In fact, there was too much free time during this period.
Example 3:
Carver was born into slavery.

Irrelevant Details

Read the paragraphs below and identify the main idea, supporting details, and irrelevant details.

Example 1

Dr. Martin Luther King, Jr., became a well-known civil rights leader because of his role in the 1955 boycott of city buses in Montgomery, Alabama. Other civil rights leaders worked on boycotts in southern cities, too. Until this time, city buses were segregated, meaning that African Americans had to sit at the back of the bus and often had to give up their seats for white people. One day, Rosa Parks refused to sit in the back of the bus, and then she refused to give up her seat for a white person. The bus was not very large. When Mrs. Parks was arrested, Dr. King led a boycott of the Montgomery buses. People who supported Dr. King and the boycott decided not to take the buses until African Americans could sit where they pleased.

Example 2

The 1950s in America were an age of prosperity, or economic well-being. The country grew stronger and its population increased. Two new states, Alaska and Hawaii, became a part of the United States. Countless new machines speeded up household chores. These machines were greatly needed. Watching television became a popular leisure, or free-time, activity. In fact, there was too much free time during this period.

Example 3

New scientific developments helped increase farm production in the 1800s. Better seeds and livestock were developed. Crop rotation and fertilizers were used to improve the soil. So much food was produced that there was a surplus. Fortunately, George Washington Carver discovered the following new uses for soybeans, peanuts, and sweet potatoes: face cream, cooking oil, tooth polish, and paint. Carver was born into slavery.

Paragraph Rip & Tear

Write the main idea and all the detail sentences for a paragraph in the spaces below. Tear out any sentences that are not supporting details.

Main Idea

Detail	Detail	Detail	Detail	Detail	Detail	Detail	Detail

Using an Equation to Find the Main Idea

Opening the Lesson

❦ I focus my students' attention on main idea and details by reading aloud pairs of sentences. Here are some examples of sentence pairs I've used in my classroom.

A. Tulips are starting to sprout out of the ground. (detail)
   Spring has finally arrived. (main idea)

B. The North won the Civil War. (main idea)
   The North had more soldiers and equipment than the South did. (detail)

C. The day was *not* peaceful. (main idea)
   The neighbor's dog barked because of the loud hammering across the street. (detail)

D. Aunt Martha and Uncle Bob brought water balloons. (detail)
   The family reunion was a huge success. (main idea)

❦ I reread each pair of sentences and then ask my students to tell me which one is the main idea and which one is a detail that supports the main idea.

Teaching the Lesson

1. Now that students have had experience in identifying irrelevant details in a paragraph, show them how to do the same thing with passages. Remind students that a passage is made up of several paragraphs about the same topic. The main idea of a passage is mentioned in the first paragraph and repeated in the last paragraph. The title will support the main idea, too.

2. Display the Bigger Picture reproducible on the overhead. Explain that the main ideas of the paragraphs in a passage are like the details that make up the main idea of the entire passage. To familiarize my students with this concept, I point to the appropriate sections of the reproducible and say the following: *The bigger picture of the passage is the main idea of the passage. Each paragraph has its own big picture with a main idea and details.*

3. Distribute the Urban Jungle passage to your students. After they read the passage, ask volunteers to identify the big picture (main idea) in each

Objective

Students find the main idea of a passage.

Reproducibles

The Bigger Picture, page 21 (Make 1 transparency.)

Main Idea Equation, page 22 (Make 1 copy for each pair.)

Urban Jungle passage, page 23 (Make 1 copy for each student.)

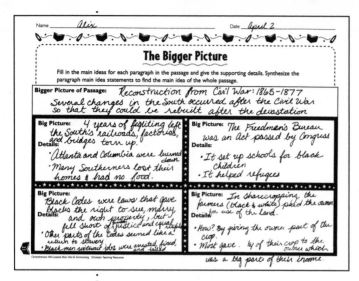

Name _Alix_ **Date** _April 2_

The Bigger Picture

Fill in the main ideas for each paragraph in the passage and give the supporting details. Synthesize the paragraph main idea statements to find the main idea of the whole passage.

Bigger Picture of Passage: _Reconstruction from Civil War: 1865–1877 Several changes in the South occurred after the Civil War so that they could be rebuilt after the devastation_

Big Picture: _4 years of fighting left the South's railroads, factories, and bridges torn up._
Details:
• _Atlanta and Columbia were burned down_
• _Many Southerners lost their homes & had no food._

Big Picture: _The Freedmen's Bureau was an Act passed by Congress_
Details:
• _It set up schools for black children_
• _It helped refugees_

Big Picture: _Black Codes were laws that gave blacks the right to sue, marry, and own property, but fell short of justice and equality_
Details:
• _Other parts of the Codes seemed like a return to slavery_
• _Black men without jobs were arrested, fined, and jailed_

Big Picture: _In sharecropping the farmers (black & white) paid the owner for use of the land._
Details:
• _How? By giving the owner part of the crop._
• _Most gave ¼ of their crop to the owner which was a big part of their income._

Name _Norma_ **Date** _December 8_

Main Idea Equation

"Add up" the topic sentences from each paragraph in the passage to find a main idea that combines all of the paragraph main idea statements.

Matter may be classified as a mixture or a substance.
(topic sentence of paragraph 1)

+

Each kind of matter in a mixture keeps its properties.
(topic sentence of paragraph 2)

+

Some mixtures are made up of several kinds of gases.
(topic sentence of paragraph 3)

+

There are several different types of mixtures.
(topic sentence of paragraph 4)

+

Substances in a mixture can be separated by physical means.
(topic sentence of paragraph 5)

=

Main Idea of Passage
Mixtures are unique blends of two or more substances. The substances do not change by being mixed and can be separated. Mixtures can be in the form of a liquid, gas, or solid.

---

paragraph. Then discuss with students what the bigger picture, or the main idea, of the passage is. Fill in the Bigger Picture transparency.

4. You can also provide another learning opportunity for your students by explaining that they can use an addition equation to find the main idea of a passage. Hand out the Main Idea Equation reproducible. Place the Main Idea Equation transparency on the overhead.

5. Then reread each paragraph aloud. Ask students to tell which sentence is the main idea of each paragraph. Remind them that this may also be called the topic sentence. Write a topic sentence on each line of the equation.

6. When you've written down all the topic sentences, ask students to tell you what the main idea of the passage is. Write it underneath the equal sign.

7. Ask students which organizer they liked the best. Allow them to choose the organizer they will use for the Assessment activity below.

Closing the Lesson

Use one or more of these activities to wrap up the mini-lesson.

✱ **Journal:** Challenge students to analyze how the Main Idea Equation graphic organizer works.

✱ **Assessment:** Choose a passage from a textbook, and direct students to find the main idea of the passage by using the Bigger Picture or the Main Idea Equation graphic organizer. They can draw the graphic organizers on paper, or you may want to make copies for them.

The Bigger Picture

Fill in the main ideas for each paragraph in the passage and give the supporting details. Synthesize the paragraph main idea statements to find the main idea of the whole passage.

Bigger Picture of Passage:

Big Picture:

Details:

Big Picture:

Details:

Big Picture:

Details:

Big Picture:

Details:

Comprehension Mini-Lessons: Main Idea & Summarizing Scholastic Teaching Resources

Main Idea Equation

"Add up" the topic sentences from each paragraph in the passage to find a main idea that combines all of the paragraph main idea statements.

+ x ÷ − + x ÷ − + x ÷ − + x ÷ − + x ÷ − + x ÷ − + x ÷ − + x ÷ − + x ÷ −

_____

(topic sentence of paragraph 1)

+

_____

(topic sentence of paragraph 2)

+

_____

(topic sentence of paragraph 3)

+

_____

(topic sentence of paragraph 4)

+

_____

(topic sentence of paragraph 5)

=

Main Idea of Passage

Comprehension Mini-Lessons: Main Idea & Summarizing Scholastic Teaching Resources

Urban Jungle

Zoos today focus on education and conservation, or saving endangered species and natural habitats. In the past few years, several of the nation's leading zoos have spent millions of dollars building new exhibits. These displays show animals living in spaces that resemble their native homes.

The panda exhibit at Zoo Atlanta raises money to save a natural habitat—bamboo forests in China. Zoo Atlanta built a $7 million habitat for Yang Yang and Lun Lun, two pandas moving there from China. This is an important exhibit because giant pandas are among the world's rarest mammals, or warm-blooded animals with backbones. Fewer than 1,000 pandas exist in China's mountains because of their diminishing food supply. Farmers have to cut down bamboo forests to clear land, eliminating the panda's major food source. A single panda must eat more than 20 pounds of the plant each day to survive. The zoo will make sure that the pandas have the food and environment they need in order to survive.

Zoos across the country help other endangered animals, including elephants, monkeys, turtles, and cranes by replicating their habitats and helping wounded animals heal. Zoo studies also help scientists learn how to breed endangered species and help them give birth to new generations. Their studies paid off at the San Diego Zoo last month where a rare, new arrival boosted the U.S. panda population from three to four. The baby panda was the first born in the U.S. in ten years.

"Zoos are now spending more time trying to understand animals," says Ed Spevak, a Bronx Zoo curator, or person in charge of the exhibit. "Zoo animals live longer in zoos because they get better care, nutrition, and doctors." And today's zoo animals serve an important function: They help preserve the lives and homes of animals living in the wild.

Comprehension Mini-Lessons: Main Idea & Summarizing Scholastic Teaching Resources

Adapted from "Urban Jungle" by Tracey Gardner. *Scholastic News*, September 20, 1999.

Time to Write!

Objective

Students create writing plans to illustrate how the topic sentences of paragraphs reflect the main idea of their essays.

Materials

paper and pen

Reproducibles

Main Idea Web, page 26 (Make 1 transparency and 1 copy for each student.)

Opening the Lesson

✿ Write a one-page essay about what your ideal school day would be like. (Now is the time to indulge your fantasies of a school utopia in a creative way!) Make transparencies of your essay and brainstorming notes that will help students see how you constructed each paragraph around a main idea.

✿ Display the transparencies. After reading aloud your essay, discuss the format and content with your students. Use the notes to show how your ideas evolved into an essay. Share your own creative struggles, and ask for—and listen to—your students' critiques of the essay.

Teaching the Lesson

1. Now it's your students' turn to write about what their ideal school day would be like. This topic is a great way for you to get to know them better, too.

2. Guide them in using the Main Idea Web graphic organizer in brainstorming ideas for their essays. Model writing main ideas for the introduction (paragraph 1). Here is an example I use with my students: *What would make my school day ideal? Well, it would have to be fun. I know! My ideal school day would take place at Disneyland.* Remind students that each paragraph must be related to the introduction.

3. Once they have brainstormed their topic sentences for the three paragraphs, students can start working on their rough drafts. (NOTE: Students may include more than three details per paragraph.)

Closing the Lesson

Use one or more of these activities to wrap up the mini-lesson.

✿ **Students Working Together:** Have students share rough drafts of their essays with partners. Make sure they look for alignment among the topic sentences and the essay's main idea. Partners can help one another by comparing the essay outline on the graphic organizer to

the completed essay. This is the time for students to check the rubric to make sure they've met the requirements.

✦ **Auditory:** After the final edit, students can write their final drafts and attach their graphic organizers to the back. Ask them to read aloud their essays and to share their creative processes with the rest of the class.

Idea

It's a good idea to create a rubric that spells out the requirements for this essay. Each rubric will differ according to which grade you teach. I include some of the following items on the rubric for my class:

• The title is creative and reflects the main idea.

• The introduction is creative and effective.

• The main idea of the essay is mentioned in the introduction.

• The topic sentence of each paragraph supports the main idea of the passage.

• The details within each paragraph support the topic sentence.

• The conclusion is creative and effective, and it repeats the main idea.

• Punctuation, grammar, and spelling are correct.

My Ideal School day – A Teacher's Perspective
by LeAnn Nickelsen

We kind of know what students would want in their ideal school day, but do you have any idea what a teacher would want? My ideal school day would consist of absolutely no discipline problems, a one-hour lunch that is catered, and a full-time assistant in the classroom. This isn't too much to ask for—is it?

First of all, an ideal school day for me would have no discipline problems. All of the students would follow the rules perfectly, fulfill their responsibilities, and be kind to everyone. Wouldn't it be neat not to have to correct a student's behavior for a whole day? Nobody would get their feelings hurt, all students would feel included, and students would be giving to their peers. There wouldn't even be peer pressure…and to think that the word *gossip* wouldn't even exist! I would get to toss out the consequences for breaking a rule, and everybody would get a full recess. I wouldn't have to spend time writing letters to students' parents or calling them. My day would be stress-free if all students followed the rules, fulfilled their responsibilities, and were kind to everyone.

Secondly, an ideal day would have a one-hour relaxing, catered lunch. Lunchtime is really a teacher's only break. Lunchtime typically consists of scarfing down food and rushing out to recess duty. We barely have the chance to call our spouses, put lipstick on, and of course, use the restroom. A one-hour lunch would allow me more time in the morning to get ready and grade papers because I wouldn't have to fix a lunch. My mouth just waters when I think of Olive Garden catering our lunches. What a great break this would be on my ideal school day.

Finally, my ideal school day would include a full-time assistant in my classroom. She would grade all papers, help me teach, answer questions so that all students' needs are met, comfort any student who felt down, run my errands, complete book orders, file my lessons, photocopy all papers, prepare all of the science labs, and tell me, "What a great lesson that was!" It would be wonderful to have such a supportive adult in the classroom. The students would love having two teachers on this ideal school day.

While I'm asking, can I have several weeks of this ideal school day? I'll promise not to assign too much homework.…

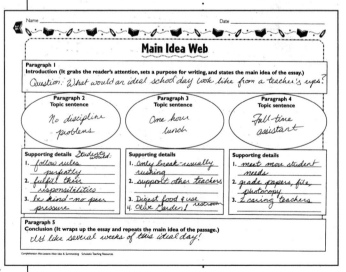

Main Idea Web

Paragraph 1
Introduction (It grabs the reader's attention, sets a purpose for writing, and states the main idea of the essay.)

Paragraph 2
Topic Sentence

Paragraph 3
Topic Sentence

Paragraph 4
Topic Sentence

Supporting Details

1.

2.

3.

Supporting Details

1.

2.

3.

Supporting Details

1.

2.

3.

Paragraph 5
Conclusion (It wraps up the essay and repeats the main idea of the passage.)

Comprehension Mini-Lessons: Main Idea & Summarizing   Scholastic Teaching Resources

Test-Taking Format

Opening the Lesson

❀ In order to show that related sentences have the same main idea, I write the following sentences on the chalkboard or on a transparency:

Detail sentences:
—Like good pals, cats enjoy curling up with you and keeping you company.
—Cats clean up after themselves, so you don't have to.
—Cats usually keep themselves occupied indoors, even when you're not around.
—Cats keep rodents out of your house.

Main idea choices:

(A) Cats are fun pals. **(C)** Cats and dogs are similar in many ways.

(B) Cats make good pets. **(D)** Cats are an expensive but great pet to own.

❀ I read aloud the detail sentences. Then, as I read aloud each of the main idea choices, I ask if the main idea relates to each detail sentence. I put a tally mark beside the main idea choice for each related detail sentence. In this way, students are voting for the best main idea choice. In the example, *A* gets only one tally mark (it's related to the first detail sentence about cats being good pals, but it's not related to any of the others), *C* and *D* get no tally marks because they contain information about cats that is unrelated to the detail sentences, and *B* receives four tally marks because "Cats make good pets" provides the big picture for every detail— all are positive statements about owning a cat as a pet.

❀ I make sure to point out to students that the topic or main idea sentences they'll find in the answer choices on a test can have the same meaning as sentences in the test passage even if they are worded differently or if their structure differs.

Teaching the Lesson

1. Tell students that they can find the main idea of paragraphs and passages in multiple-choice tests by counting the related sentences in the text. The answer choice that has the most related sentences is correct.

Objective

Students use a tallying strategy to find the main idea in sample test passages.

Reproducibles

Main Idea Paragraphs, page 29 (Make 1 transparency.)

Main Idea Passage, page 30 (Make 1 copy for each student.)

Tip

Organize the reading by having students number the paragraphs of the passage in order. This helps when they want to refer back to the passage: "In paragraph four I found…"

Tip

Make a poster or transparency of the R-E-A-D steps so that students can refer to them.

2. Place the Main Idea Paragraphs transparency on the overhead and ask students to read Paragraph 1. Then walk them through the steps below to find the main idea of this paragraph.

R—Read the entire paragraph or passage first.

E—Evaluate each answer choice. Which sentences in the paragraph or passage are related to the answer choice? Put a tally mark next to the answer choice for each related sentence you find in the passage.

A—Add up the tally marks to find which answer choice has the most votes. That choice is the main idea of the paragraph or passage. If two or more answer choices have the same number of tally marks, reread the paragraph or passage to see which answer choice relates best to the whole paragraph or passage.

D—Double check by answering the following questions:

• Does my answer choice give the big picture? Or is it a general statement? (It should not be a detail.)

• Is my answer choice a topic sentence that has many details to support it?

• Is my answer choice mentioned in the first and last paragraphs of the passage?

• Is the title related to the main idea of the passage?

3. Have your class use the R-E-A-D steps to find the main idea of Paragraph 2 on the overhead. Get students involved by calling on volunteers to lead the class through the different steps.

4. Make sure students notice the different ways main idea questions may be phrased on tests. For example, "What is this passage mostly about?" doesn't even contain the phrase *main idea*.

Closing the Lesson

Use one or more of these activities to wrap up the mini-lesson.

✤ **Journal:** Ask students to write their own explanations of how to find the main idea of a paragraph or passage on a multiple-choice test by using the tally mark system to quantify their answers.

✤ **Assessment:** Have students use the steps to complete the Main Idea Passage reproducible.

Answers
Main Idea Paragraphs, page 29: Paragraph 1: C; Paragraph 2: D
Main Idea Passage, page 30: 1. B; 2. C; 3. D

Main Idea Paragraphs

Read each passage. Then choose the best answer for the question that follows.

Paragraph 1

In 1998 Tom Whitaker made history. He became the first disabled person to climb Mount Everest—one of the most dangerous and challenging mountains to climb in the world. Ten years earlier, Tom was badly injured in a car accident. He lost his right foot and his kneecap. Still, Tom wasn't going to let anything keep him from his goal. He was going to climb the world's tallest mountain.

This paragraph is mainly about—

(A) how people avoid knee injuries

(B) why Mount Everest is too dangerous to climb

(C) a disabled person who climbs Mount Everest

(D) a serious car accident that injured a young man

Paragraph 2

In the summer of 1997, a disaster struck Indonesia. A series of fires sent huge clouds of smoke into the air. The fires spread across a vast area and destroyed thousands of acres. But it wasn't the flames that caused the most serious problems. It was the smoke, which was so thick that it made people sick. Even people living hundreds of miles away from the fire were affected.

What is this paragraph mostly about?

(A) Smoke from fires made many people sick.

(B) Huge clouds of smoke were everywhere.

(C) Smoke is bad for your health.

(D) Fires harmed land and people in Indonesia.

  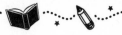

Main Idea Passage

They look like blobs of jelly. They sting like bees, and they appeared in record numbers off the U.S. shores last summer. On the Atlantic and Pacific coasts, swimmers reported more jellyfish sightings, and stingings, than ever before.

"I was swimming and I felt something like a bee sting on my thigh," says Terryn Marrette, 9, of Maryland, who ran into a jellyfish at a Connecticut beach in August. In San Diego, California, bathers steered clear of huge, purple jellyfish called *Chrysaora achlyos*. They have bodies the size of basketballs and 25-foot stinging tentacles. This was the first sighting of these slimy giants since 1989.

Researchers have some theories about why the numbers are up, but there is no clear answer. This summer's hot, dry weather could be the cause of the jellyfish invasion. "Maybe the water temperature around shore was just right," says Leslee Yasukochi of Birch Aquarium in La Jolla, California. Warmer than usual shallow waters may also have offered more food. Jellyfish dine on tiny shrimp, fish, and microscopic sea life.

"They have no brains, yet they can do everything an animal needs to do. They swim, eat food, and find mates," says Denise Breitberg, a biologist at the Academy of Natural Sciences in St. Leonard, Maryland. Jellies have no heart or gills, and are made mostly of water. The sting from the man-of-war can be deadly, but the sting from most jellies is just irritating. Some creatures, such as sea turtles and humans, snack on them. Jellyfish have fascinated researchers for years—and now there may be more opportunities than ever to study the creatures.

Adapted from "Jellyfish Invasion," by Christine Puelo. *Scholastic News*, November 1, 1999

1. What is the main idea of the first paragraph?

(A) Jellyfish look like blobs of jelly.

(B) An increase in jellyfish has been reported along U.S. coasts.

(C) Maryland had at least one jellyfish sighting.

(D) The sting of a jellyfish is like a bee sting.

2. What is the third paragraph mainly about?

(A) Shallow water contains more food for jellyfish.

(B) The water temperature was just right for jellyfish to survive.

(C) Hot, dry weather may have created the perfect water environment for a jellyfish invasion.

(D) Jellyfish eat shrimp, fish, and microscopic sea life.

3. What is the fourth paragraph mostly about?

(A) Jellyfish are made up mostly of water.

(B) It's amazing that humans would eat jellyfish.

(C) Man-of-war stings can kill humans.

(D) Many researchers find jellyfish fascinating to study.

Comprehension Mini-Lessons: Main Idea & Summarizing   Scholastic Teaching Resources

Putting It All Together: Main Idea Information Books

Preparing for the Project

❖ You will need to choose six different reading passages for students to base their projects on. I like to choose a variety of topics that will appeal to them, such as the Civil War, planets, pets, and so on.

❖ Hang a calendar chart with project due dates in the classroom. The calendar should include deadlines for individual pages and for the entire project. I allot one booklet page per class period and then I check them the next day for completion and quality.

❖ Since students choose which reproducibles to use on pages 4 and 5 of their booklets, you will need to create a sign-up sheet so that they can indicate which reproducibles they want to use.

❖ Create a sample booklet for students to refer to as they work.

Introducing the Project

1. Explain to students that they will be creating booklets to summarize what they've learned about main idea. Display your sample booklet. Keep it available for students to study.

2. As you model the construction of a booklet, have students complete the steps with you. Align the three sheets of construction paper, and then fold them in half to create a 12-page booklet that measures 9 inches by 12 inches. Staple the pages together along the fold. (You may also staple together six smaller sheets of construction paper along one of the long edges.)

3. Distribute the Student Project Sheets and discuss the directions. Make sure everyone understands how to do the project.

Assessing the Project

❖ **Presentation:** Invite students to share their projects with the class. Let them choose which part of their booklets they would like to present (or have presented). Most students like to share their stories on page 7.

❖ **Assessment:** Use the Main Idea Information Book rubric on page 34 to grade the projects. Attach a rubric to the back of each student's booklet.

Objective

Students review different ways to find the main idea and create an information booklet about a topic of interest.

Materials

3 sheets of 12- by 18-inch construction paper for each student, markers, stapler, glue, 6 different reading passages, calendar chart, sign-up sheet, sample booklet

Reproducibles

Reproducibles (Make 1 copy for each student.)*:
Student Project Sheets, pages 32–33; The Big Picture, page 9; Paragraph Rip & Tear, page 18; Main Idea on the Table, page 14; The Bigger Picture, page 21; Main Idea Equation, page 22; Main Idea Web, page 26; Main Idea Information Book Rubric, page 34

*NOTE: Based on student choices, you'll need additional copies of some reproducibles.

Main Idea Information Books
Student Project Sheet

Cover Page
Write the passage title, your name, and the date. Draw a picture on the cover to illustrate your topic.

Table of Contents
Complete this page last. Don't forget to number pages 1–8!

Introduction
Write a paragraph that explains the difference between main idea and details. Then write a sample paragraph of 5 or 6 sentences about any topic.

Page 1
Choose a paragraph from the passage you've chosen. Use it to complete the Big Picture reproducible. Glue the completed reproducible to this page.

Page 2
Select a different paragraph from the passage. Use it to complete the Paragraph Rip & Tear reproducible. Glue the completed reproducible to this page.

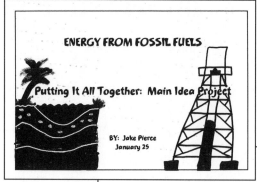

ENERGY FROM FOSSIL FUELS

Putting It All Together: Main Idea Project

BY: Jake Pierce
January 25

TABLE OF CONTENTS

INTRODUCTION
The Difference Between Main Idea and Details

Main Idea + Details = Paragraph

A paragraph is made up of sentences that are about the same event or topic. Most of the sentences within the paragraph are mostly about the same thing. The main idea is what the paragraph is mostly about. Details are the sentences that describe the main idea of a paragraph. The details and main idea are lumped together in one paragraph. Details are specific events while the main ideas are general, big events.

An example of a well-written paragraph:

My dog, Ritzy, sure does like to bark a lot during the day. She gets so angry with the squirrels that she must think that her bark is like a little spanking to them for coming into our yard. If it rains or thunders, she must think that her bark will scare away the weather because she looks up into the sky and barks until it stops. When another dog walks by our house, she must think that all of the land within her vision belongs to her and her only because she barks constantly when another dog even comes near our house. Ritzy is a great dog, but I guess the Shelti...

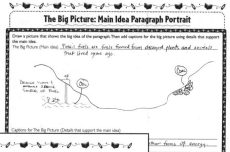

The Big Picture: Main Idea Paragraph Portrait

Draw a picture that shows the big idea of the paragraph. Then add captions for the big picture using details that support the main idea.
The Big Picture (Main idea) Fossil fuels are fuels formed from decayed plants and animals that lived years ago.

Captions for The Big Picture (Details that support the main idea)

...ther forms of energy.

Paragraph Rip & Tear

Write the main idea and all the detail sentences for a paragraph in the spaces below. Tear out any sentences that are not supporting details.

Main Idea
Coal is formed over millions of years, deep below the earth's surface

Detail	Detail	Detail	Detail	Detail	Detail	Detail	Detail	Detail

Comprehension Mini-Lessons: Main Idea & Summarizing   Scholastic Teaching Resources

Page 3

Choose another paragraph from the passage. Use it to complete the Main Idea on the Table graphic organizer reproducible. Glue the completed reproducible to this page.

Page 4

Select a different paragraph from the passage. Look at the reproducibles your teacher has. Choose your favorite reproducible. Complete it using the paragraph. Glue the completed reproducible to this page.

Page 5

Find the main idea of the entire passage. Complete the Main Idea Equation or Bigger Picture reproducible. Glue the completed reproducible to this page.

Pages 6–7

Write a fiction or nonfiction story about a character or person in the passage. Use the Main Idea Web to brainstorm your ideas. (Go through the steps of the writing process with this piece of writing.) Glue the completed reproducible to page 6. Attach your story to page 7.

Page 8

Write a paragraph about how learning about the main idea and details has helped you become a better writer and reader. Then write a paragraph about which strategies you will use in the future to find the main ideas of paragraphs and passages. Explain why these strategies work for you.

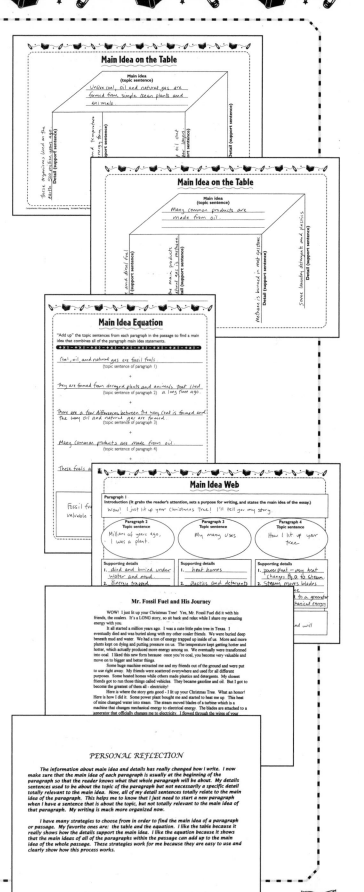

Main Idea Information Book Rubric

Student's Name _____ Date _____

CRITERIA	Incomplete 0	Okay 1	Good 2	Outstanding 3

Assignment

1. Cover, table of contents, and introduction pages:
   The cover includes your name, title of passage, date, and illustration of passage. The table of contents lists all pages in the booklet with titles and corresponding page numbers. The introduction includes the main idea paragraph and the sample paragraph.

2. Page 1: The Big Picture reproducible is completed and attached.

3. Page 2: The Paragraph Rip & Tear reproducible is completed and attached. The paragraph used is different from the paragraph on page 1.

4. Page 3: The Main Idea on the Table reproducible is completed and attached. The paragraph used is different from the paragraphs on pages 1–2.

5. Page 4: Student choice reproducible is completed and attached. The paragraph used is different from the paragraphs on pages 1–3.

6. Page 5: The Main Idea Equation or Bigger Picture reproducible is completed and attached. The paragraph used is different from the paragraphs on pages 1–4.

7. Pages 6–7: The Main Idea Web reproducible is completed and attached. It has a story based on a character or person from the passage attached to page 7.

8. Page 8: Features one paragraph about how main idea and details make you a better writer and reader and one paragraph about which strategies you will use to identify main idea and details. This last paragraph explains why the strategies work for you.

9. Overall understanding of main idea and details

Things you did well:

Opportunities for growth:

TOTAL SCORE: _____ /27

Comprehension Mini-Lessons: Main Idea & Summarizing Scholastic Teaching Resources

Summarizing

Hand Summaries

Opening the Lesson

❋ The focus of this activity is to identify the elements of a summary. I bring in a short newspaper article with a focused lead paragraph that will be interesting to my students. For example, when we were studying the ocean, I used an article on sharks.

❋ I ask my students to listen carefully and to write down any important words or phrases that will help them retell the news story to a curious friend.

❋ As we discuss their responses, I list their words and phrases on the chalkboard.

❋ Then we circle the words that tell who the article was about, star the words that tell what the article was about, underline the when and where descriptions, and draw a box around the why and how it happened phrases. Anything remaining that's not useful, we cross out.

❋ Together we synthesize and write a summary statement using the remaining key elements of who, what, when, where, why, and how.

❋ We return to the news article and compare our summary statement to the lead paragraph, which is often a complete summary. Students check that all the elements are present.

> **Tip** ·
>
> With students who grasp main idea, I model my own thinking about how to summarize, explaining: *I can use what I know about the main idea and details of the article to summarize it; I look for the big picture, write it in a sentence, and make this the topic sentence of my summary. Then I select only important details to support that main idea sentence. When I reread my summary, I check that I have included information about who, what, when, where, why, and how.*

Teaching the Lesson

1. To begin the lesson, draw and label a copy of the Hand Summary reproducible on the chalkboard (or you may make and display the poster mentioned in the tip on page 37).

Objective

Students learn that a good summary tells who, what, where, when, why, and how.

Materials

newspaper articles, posterboard, stapler or paper clips, markers (optional)

Reproducibles

Hand Summary, page 38 (Make 1 double-sided copy for each pair.)

Hand Summary Organizer, page 39 (Make 1 double-sided copy for each pair and 1 copy for each student.)

2. Explain that the hand contains the elements of a good summary. For example, I say to my class: *A good summary tells who did what, where, when, why, and how. The elements don't have to be presented in this order, but they should appear in the order in which they occur in the article or story you're summarizing. And sometimes, not every element will appear in a summary. For example, how something happened may not be mentioned in an article or story.*

3. Pass out copies of the Hand Summary and Hand Summary Sheet reproducibles to pairs of students. Also give them newspaper articles or allow them to select their own articles to summarize.

4. Although your students will work collaboratively to gather the information, have each complete a Hand Summary: One student jots notes about the most important information on the Hand Summary and fills in the first six boxes on the Hand Summary sheet. This student then writes the summary on his or her own. The other student acts as coach after the summary is complete by asking the following questions:

- *Why did you choose to put the information in this order?*
- *Could you rearrange the sentences in any way to make the summary clearer?*
- *Are any of the elements of a good summary missing? Was that information mentioned in the article?*

The coach also proofreads the summary.

5. Students then switch roles and write summaries of new articles. Remind pairs to staple or paper-clip their articles and reproducibles together and hand them in to you.

Closing the Lesson

Use one or more of these activities to wrap up the mini-lesson.

✸ **Journal:** Ask students to explain what a summary is and what to include in a good summary. Then have them put their knowledge to the test by writing a summary of what they did yesterday after dinner.

✸ **Assessment:** Distribute copies of the Hand Summary sheet and any passage or short story. Tell your students to write a summary of the work.

✸ **Students Working Together:** After you pair or group students, let them complete a Venn Diagram by comparing and contrasting summary and main idea.

Tip

How to make a Hand Summary poster: Using a transparency of the reproducible on page 38 and an overhead projector, project a poster-sized hand outline onto posterboard taped to the wall. Trace the outline on the posterboard with permanent marker and fill in the title and labels on each finger and the palm.

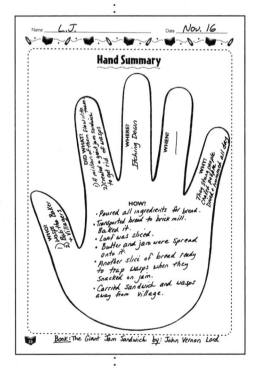

Hand Summary

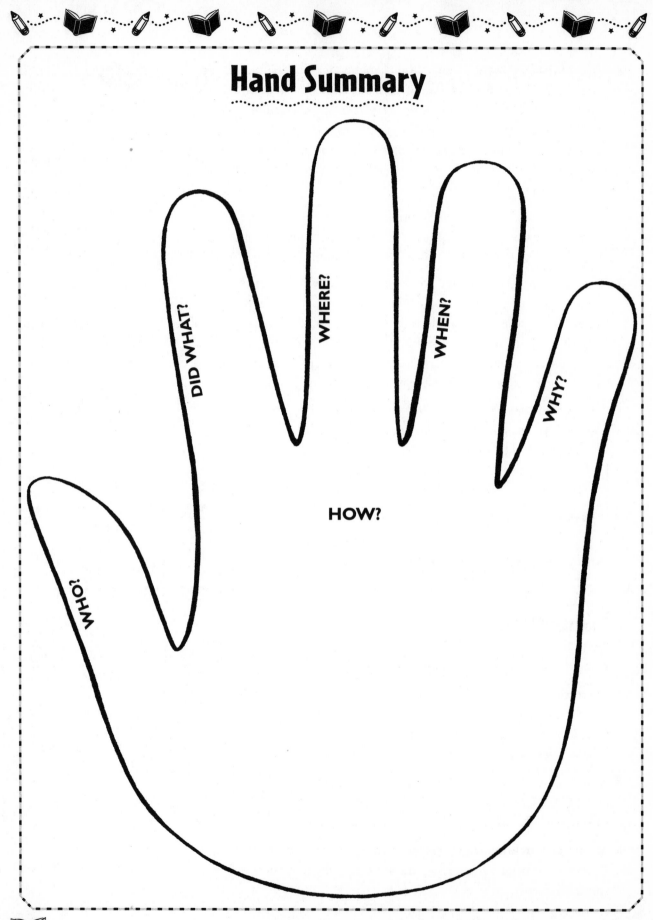

Hand Summary Organizer

WHO?

DID WHAT?

WHERE?

WHEN?

WHY?

HOW?

SUMMARY

_____

_____

_____

_____

_____

A Title's Worth a Thousand Words

Objective

Students title pictures to help them create summaries for paragraphs.

Materials

photographs from various sources (newspapers, magazines, books, book covers, calendars, and so on); *Lightning* by Seymour Simon (Scholastic, 1997) or a similar book with interesting photographs; newspaper articles

Reproducibles

Lightning Paragraphs, page 42 (Make 1 transparency.)

A Title's Worth a Thousand Words, page 43 (Make 1 copy for each student.)

Opening the Lesson

✤ For this activity, I like to use photographs that relate to topics we're currently studying in the classroom. As I show a picture, I ask my students to write down a title for it. I point out that a title doesn't have to be a complete thought or a complete sentence. The important thing is to capture the key elements of who, what, when, where, why, and how and express their personal feeling about the picture.

✤ Next I allow time for my students to write two or three sentences about why they chose that particular title. I encourage them to share their titles and reasons.

✤ Finally I share this information with my students: *You have just created summaries by looking at the photograph, making inferences about it, and then condensing the information into a few words. Very short summaries can become titles.*

Teaching the Lesson

1. This activity will show students how to choose the best title for a paragraph. I use the book *Lightning* by Seymour Simon in my classroom because it has incredible photographs that captivate my students.

2. Display the *Lightning* Paragraphs transparency on the overhead. Each paragraph paraphrases fascinating information from the book and is followed by three titles, which I created. (NOTE: If you want to focus on a different topic, you'll need to create a transparency that presents three paragraphs adapted from a related nonfiction book, and three possible titles for each one. One title should be a more effective summary than the other two choices, which might focus on a specific detail in the paragraph or something about the topic that is unrelated to the paragraph.)

3. Your students will select the best title for each paragraph. They'll also explain why they chose that title. To guide my students through the practice, I might say: *"After I read aloud the paragraph and show you the photograph that goes with it, look at the three possible titles. Decide which one is the best title for the paragraph. Why do you think that title is better than others?"* Have students repeat this process for the remaining paragraphs.

4. Now students get to practice on their own. Pair them, and hand out the A Title's Worth a Thousand Words reproducible. You can continue to use the same book or switch to a new one. Read aloud a paragraph, show the accompanying photograph, and ask pairs to write a title. I usually read four or five paragraphs to them.

5. To extend the activity, I select another four or five paragraphs from the book and let pairs create the titles on their own.

Name ___AJ___ Date ___2/27___

A Title's Worth a Thousand Words

Paragraph 1 title ___Large Sea Animal in Danger___

Paragraph 2 title ___Manatees Make the Endangered Species List___

Paragraph 3 title ___Manatees Visit Aquariums___

Paragraph 4 title ___Florida Welcomes New Laws to Protect Manatees___

Paragraph 5 title ___What You Can Do To Save Manatees___

Paragraph 6 title ___Adopt A Manatee___

Paragraph 7 title _____

Paragraph 8 title _____

Paragraph 9 title _____

Paragraph 10 title _____

Closing the Lesson

Use one or more of these activities to wrap up the mini-lesson.

✱ **Assessment:** Ask students to explain how they summarized one of the paragraphs in a title.

✱ **Visual:** Gather a variety of newspaper articles and cut off the headlines. Be sure to keep the headlines. Challenge students to read an article and then create a headline for it. Let them compare their headlines to the actual ones.

Answers
Lightning Paragraphs, page 41: 1. B; 2. A; 3. C

Lightning Paragraphs

Lightning bolts flash across the sky at over 60,000 miles per second! That speed would take you around the earth in about 25 minutes. Single bolts of lightning are about an inch wide and travel on twisted paths in the air, stretching from 6 to 10 miles in length.

Choose the best title.

(A) Long Lightning

(B) The Speed of Lightning

(C) Traveling through the Sky

In a millionth of one second, a lightning bolt flashes with the brightness of ten million one-hundred-watt lightbulbs. The pulse of energy is equal to all the power generated in all electrical generating plants in America in that split second. Because the pulse is so short, the actual energy released is much smaller and would power one lightbulb for only one month.

Choose the best title.

(A) The Power of a Lightning Bolt

(B) Lightning Is the Future Electricity

(C) Light Bright

Have you ever felt your hair stand on end right before a lightning storm? Lightning begins with rapidly moving raindrops and ice crystals in clouds. The motion results in an electrical charge buildup in the cloud. An opposite charge builds on the ground below the cloud. This is what may cause your hair to rise.

Choose the best title.

(A) Electrical Charges Strike Again

(B) Ice Crystals and Raindrops

(C) The Beginnings of Lightning

Comprehension Mini-Lessons: Main Idea & Summarizing Scholastic Teaching Resources

A Title's Worth a Thousand Words

Paragraph 1 title _____

Paragraph 2 title _____

Paragraph 3 title _____

Paragraph 4 title _____

Paragraph 5 title _____

Paragraph 6 title _____

Paragraph 7 title _____

Paragraph 8 title _____

Paragraph 9 title _____

Paragraph 10 title _____

Get to the Point

Objective

Students identify information from the beginning, middle, and end of a story and use a graphic organizer to create a summary.

Materials

Wump World by Bill Peet (Scholastic, 1970) or a similar book, short story from an anthology or textbook, paper and pens

Reproducibles

Get to the Point, page 46 (Make 1 transparency and 1 copy for each student.)

Opening the Lesson

✤ For this activity, I like to use Bill Peet's *Wump World*. If you decide to share another book or story with a simple plot line, mark the beginning, middle, and end of the work.

✤ I read aloud the beginning of *Wump World* and stop after page 15. Then I ask my students to quickly write down on a sheet of notebook paper the most important information in the beginning of the story. I give them about two minutes to write one or two sentences. (NOTE: Their names do not appear on their papers.)

✤ I repeat this process for the middle (page 27 of *Wump World*) and the end of the book.

✤ When my students have completed their "quick writes," I collect their papers. At this point, I emphasize that they will probably have some different ideas about what information was the most important in the story. None of the summaries they write will be *exactly* alike, but the summaries should include the same main ideas and major details.

✤ I randomly select a student's paper and use it to create a three- or four-sentence summary of *Wump World*, which I write on the chalkboard. Then I ask the class to evaluate the summary: *Does this summary include the most important information in the story? Does it really tell us what the story is about? Is there any information we could add or subtract?*

✤ I continue writing summaries from the "quick writes" and asking the class to assess them so everyone will see the differences, both subtle and major, in their summaries.

Teaching the Lesson

1. Display the Get to the Point transparency on the overhead. Ask students how this graphic organizer relates to what they did in the opening activity.

2. Then read aloud a short story that you have divided into three parts—beginning, middle, and end. Stop at the end of each part so that students can record the most important information on notebook paper. Take the time to talk about this information with them. There may be disagreements, but the discussion should help students weed out any unimportant information. Remind them to update the information on their paper.

3. Ask students to work together in groups of three or four to write their own three- or four-sentence summaries based on the "quick write." Circulate among them to guide the practice.

4. Invite the groups to share their summaries. Point out the subtle differences in wording but emphasize that they include the gist and major details of the story.

5. Challenge groups to develop the shortest summary possible that still includes all the necessary information. This will prepare them for the brief 1–3 sentence summaries they will encounter on the standardized test.

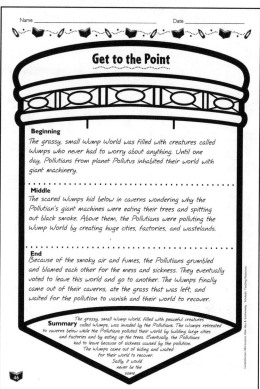

Name _____ Date _____

Get to the Point

Beginning
The grassy, small Wump World was filled with creatures called Wumps who never had to worry about anything. Until one day, Pollutians from planet Pollutus inhabited their world with giant machinery.

Middle
The scared Wumps hid below in caverns wondering why the Pollutian's giant machines were eating their trees and spitting out black smoke. Above them, the Pollutians were polluting the Wump World by creating huge cities, factories, and wastelands.

End
Because of the smoky air and fumes, the Pollutians grumbled and blamed each other for the mess and sickness. They eventually voted to leave this world and go to another. The Wumps finally came out of their caverns, ate the grass that was left, and waited for the pollution to vanish and their world to recover.

Summary The grassy, small Wump World, filled with peaceful creatures called Wumps, was invaded by the Pollutians. The Wumps retreated to caverns below while the Pollutians polluted their world by building large cities and factories and by eating up the trees. Eventually, the Pollutians had to leave because of sickness caused by the pollution. The Wumps came out of hiding and waited for their world to recover. Sadly, it would never be the same.

46

Closing the Lesson

Use one or more of these activities to wrap up the mini-lesson.

✾ **Journal:** Ask your students: *Why do you think this lesson was important for you as a reader?* Students should be able to articulate in their own words that summarizing requires them to consolidate information as they read and retell the story in their own words, which will give them a better overall understanding of the text. This activity will help students synthesize the most important information in this lesson.

✾ **Assessment:** Hand out a copy of the Get to the Point reproducible to each student. Select one or more stories from anthologies or textbooks for them to read. This time, students get to determine the beginning, middle, and end of the story. Then have them do a "quick write" to capture the most important information and create their own summaries.

Get to the Point

Beginning

Middle

End

Summary

Comprehension Mini-Lessons: Main Idea & Summarizing Scholastic Teaching Resources

PROVE It!

Opening the Lesson

✿ I tell my students that they're going to learn five steps for writing a good summary. To pique their curiosity, I reveal that the first letter of each step spells the word *PROVE*. I write the letters in a vertical line on the chalkboard.

✿ Then I challenge my students to think about what they have learned so far about writing good summaries. I ask, *What do you think each letter stands for? For instance, what could the letter P stand for?*

✿ As they brainstorm, I write their responses on the chalkboard. I usually allow about five minutes for this and then move on to teach the body of the lesson.

Teaching the Lesson

1. Put the PROVE It! transparency on the overhead, and have students compare the steps to their responses. Be sure to celebrate their correct predictions.

2. Explain each step to your students. For example, you might say:

The P stands for Predict and preview the passage. *Look at the cover— illustrations, title, subtitle, author's name, and so on. Look inside for chapter titles, pictures, boldface words, graphs, and so on. Then predict what the passage is about.*

The R stands for Read the passage.

The O stands for Organize the information. *You've learned different ways to organize information. Think about the hand summary, other graphic organizers, outlines, mindmaps, and charts. Use the method that's most helpful to you in selecting the most important information.*

The V stands for Validate and verify. *Once the information is organized, you can write the summary. You validate your summary by asking yourself whether the summary focuses on the most important information in the passage and making sure each sentence of the summary supports the big picture.*

Objective

Students use five basic steps to write a great summary

Materials

Two-Minute Mysteries by Donald Sobol (Scott Foresman, 1991) or a similar book, paper and pens

Reproducibles

PROVE It!, page 49 (Make 1 transparency and 1 copy for each pair.)

PROVE It! Rubric, page 50 (Make 1 copy for each student.)

The E *stands for* Edit. *Nobody writes a great summary the first time. You may need to add or subtract information to make sure you included all the main ideas and major details. You'll definitely have to check your spelling, capitalization, punctuation, and grammar. (This is the section that will be graded.)*

3. Use a story from *Two-Minute Mysteries* or another book to model the five steps for your students. Begin by holding up the book and talking about an element on the cover. Invite students to participate in previewing and predicting. Then read aloud the story and, with your students' help, fill in the boxes on the transparency. Aim for a summary that has a total of four to seven sentences.

4. Now pairs of students will have a chance to practice the five steps together. Hand out a copy of the PROVE It! reproducible to each pair and a short mystery or story. You may want to have them take turns completing the boxes; for instance, Maria completes *P*, Jason completes *R* and *O*, and so on. The partner who is not writing in a box should act as a coach. Move around the room to guide your students. When they seem stuck, prompt them with questions.

5. When all the pairs have completed the reproducible, review the five steps again. Then ask partners to share their work with the rest of the class. I find that this discussion really helps my students better understand the steps to developing a good summary.

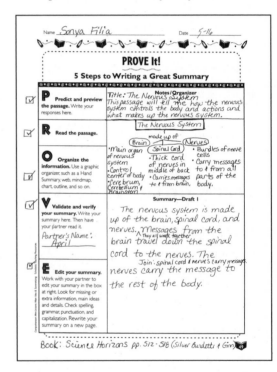

Closing the Lesson

Use one or more of these activities to wrap up the mini-lesson.

✤ **Journal:** Challenge students to write brief paragraphs that show what each step means in the summary writing process. Here is an example of a student answer that explains how the student thinks about the prediction step: *The P reminds me to preview the book—to look at the pictures, titles, and other visual things. This helps me predict what the book might be about. This is an important step in summarizing because I will pay more attention while I read to see if my prediction is right.*

✤ **Assessment:** After students read a short story and complete the PROVE It! reproducible on their own, have them use the rubric to assess their summaries. Be sure to let them preview and discuss the rubric first. You may also elect to use the rubric to grade the summaries yourself.

PROVE It!

5 Steps to Writing a Great Summary

	Notes/Organizer
Predict and preview the passage. Write your responses here.	
R **Read the passage.**	
Organize the information. Use a graphic organizer, such as a Hand Summary, web, mindmap, chart, outline, and so on.	
V **Validate and verify your summary.** Write your summary here. Then have your partner read it.	**Summary—Draft 1**
Edit your summary. Work with your partner to edit your summary in the box at right. Look for missing or extra information, main ideas, and details. Check spelling, grammar, punctuation, and capitalization. Rewrite your summary on a new page.	

PROVE It! Rubric

Student's Name _____ Date _____

CRITERIA	Incomplete 0	Okay 1	Good 2	Excellent 3
Assignment				
1. The summary reflects the title, headings, and/or subheadings of the text in some way.				
2. The first sentence of the summary is the main idea of the passage.				
3. The other sentences (3–5 sentences) are the most important details from the passage.				
4. The summary includes important information from the beginning, middle, and end of the passage.				
5. The entire summary does the job of explaining in a concise manner what the passage is about.				
Style and Structure				
6. Spelling, grammar, punctuation, and capitalization are correct.				
7. The summary contains some compound and complex sentences that combine ideas in a concise way.				

Things you did well:

Opportunities for growth:

TOTAL SCORE: _____ /21

Comprehension Mini-Lessons: Main Idea & Summarizing Scholastic Teaching Resources

Test-Taking Format

Opening the Lesson

✿ To prepare my students for reading test passages and choosing the best summaries of them, we review the different strategies they've learned to apply to summarization—hand summaries (who did what, when, where, how, and why); summing up a paragraph or passage with a title; "quick writes" that focus on beginning, middle, and end; and the five steps outlined in PROVE It!

✿ After pairing students, I challenge them to take two minutes to write down the qualities of a good summary. This is a short brainstorming session.

✿ As we discuss the qualities they've described, I create a list on the chalkboard. Here's an example of a list I compiled with my students' input.

> A good summary—
> • reflects the title or subheadings in some way.
> • has the main idea of the passage in the first sentence.
> • includes important details from the passage in the other sentences.
> • explains what the entire passage is about.
> • is written in your own words.
> • is brief.
> • contains important information about the beginning, middle, and end of the passage.
> • ends with a closing sentence.

✿ We discuss which of these criteria would be useful for evaluating multiple-choice summary statements on a test passage. From our discussion I select three to five points from the list and create a summary checklist for students to use as they eliminate answer choices on test passages.

Teaching the Lesson

1. Place a transparency of An Unexpected Ending on the overhead and read aloud the passage. Then think aloud to show students how you

Objective
Students choose the best summary for test passages.

Materials
passages from textbooks or another source

Reproducibles
An Unexpected Ending (fiction passage), page 53 (Make 1 transparency.)

Good-Bye to the Mir Space Station (nonfiction passage), page 54 (Make 1 copy for each student.)

might approach the answer choices. For instance, I might say, *I think the main idea of this passage is that a reader got a big surprise when he or she reached the end of a book. That's also mentioned in the title. I'll look to see if any of the answer choices mention that main idea.* My students find that *D* is the choice with the main idea and title reflected in the first sentence.

2. Continue modeling until you have narrowed down the answer choices to the correct one. (NOTE: When I model the process of eliminating incorrect answer choices, I go down our summary checklist and show how the correct choice meets the criteria while the other choices do not. I also ask my students if they agree with me. This discussion helps me focus on students who may need more practice. At the same time, giving and listening to reasons for their answer choices benefits the entire class.)

3. Hand out the copies of the nonfiction passage reproducible so that students can work on their own. If you have created a checklist, make sure it is available to students as a poster or a reference page. Set a time limit for them to read the passage and find the best summary.

Closing the Lesson

Use one or more of these activities to wrap up the mini-lesson.

✤ **Auditory:** Ask volunteers to explain the processes they used in selecting the best summary.

✤ **Journal:** Ask students to answer the following question: *Which strategies did you use, and why?*

✤ **Students Working Together:** Select two passages from your students' textbooks or from another source. Pair students, and give a different passage to each partner. Challenge them to create their own answer choices for a summarizing test on the passages. The partners will then take each other's tests.

Answers
An Unexpected Ending, page 53: D
Good-Bye to the Mir Space Station, page 54: A

Tip
Point out to students that the summaries on tests may be shorter than the summaries they have been writing.

52

An Unexpected Ending

All week long, I looked forward to finishing the book I was reading. It was called "The Secret of the Hidden Cave," and it was a mystery, which is my favorite kind of book. Since I was so busy with homework, I knew I wouldn't be able to finish the book until Friday. It was the most exciting book I'd ever read, and I couldn't wait to finish it.

Friday rolled around at last. I sat down on the couch and began to read. Each page was better than the one before. What would the explorers find when they finally reached the bottom of the cave? The question was driving me crazy! Finally I only had three more pages to go. I was about to learn the secret of the hidden cave! I turned the page. I couldn't believe my eyes! The last page was missing!

"It's not fair!" I yelled.

Then I heard laughter. My little sister was standing in front of me. She was waving the missing page in her hand.

After solving the mystery of the missing page, which I did by catching my sister and retrieving the page, I sat down on the couch again. I took a deep breath and then discovered what the explorers had found.

What is the best summary for this passage? Choose the best answer.

(A) A reader is eager to finish reading a mystery. Unfortunately, too much homework gets in the way. He can't finish the book until Friday.

(B) A book tells about explorers diving to the bottom of a cave. The last page of the book is missing. The reader can't finish the book.

(C) A girl tears the last page out of a mystery book. She is unable to hide what she did. Her deed is discovered.

(D) A reader sits down to finish an exciting book. He or she finds out the last page is missing. Luckily, the reader rescues the page and can finish the book.

Comprehension Mini-Lessons: Main Idea & Summarizing   Scholastic Teaching Resources

Good-Bye to the Mir Space Station

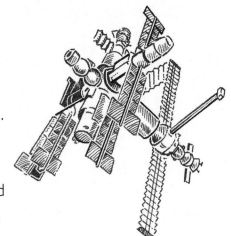

March of 2001 was a sad month for the Russian space program. After thirteen-and-a-half years, and more than 86,000 orbits, the space station Mir was finally brought back to Earth. It plunged into the Pacific Ocean on March 23, 2001.

Mir had been in space since 1986. For years, the station was the pride of the Russian space program. It was a home to both Russian and American astronauts who conducted experiments in space. Increasingly, however, Mir had become the scene of accidents. Three serious accidents occurred within a single year, 1997. First a fire broke out on board. The crew almost had to leave the space station. Then a cargo ship crashed into the side of Mir, which damaged the station's solar panels. Finally a computer breakdown nearly caused a disaster.

In the end, none of these accidents caused the shutdown of Mir. The space station was abandoned simply because it was too old. The equipment was breaking down and trash littered the station. Astronauts who stayed at Mir would probably be risking their lives. Despite all this, the space station lasted five years longer than it was expected to—and helped us make progress in our understanding of space.

What is the best summary for this passage? Choose the best answer.

(A) Mir spent many years in space. Astronauts conducted space experiments on it. But the space station had to be abandoned because it was too old.

(B) Fire broke out on the Mir space station. Then the crew almost had to abandon it. Finally a cargo ship crashed into its side.

(C) The Mir space station was so old that equipment kept breaking. Trash littered it. Astronauts might be risking their lives to visit it.

(D) Mir was launched into space in 1986. Russian and American astronauts lived at the station. They conducted experiments in space.

Comprehension Mini-Lessons: Main Idea & Summarizing   Scholastic Teaching Resources

Putting It All Together: Summarizing A Favorite Book

Preparing for the Project

✿ Your students will base their final projects on a book of fiction they select. You may want to provide a list of possible titles or make a variety of books available to them.

✿ In the classroom, hang a calendar chart with project due dates. The calendar should include deadlines for individual pages and for the entire project. I allot one page per class period and then check them the next day for completion and quality.

✿ Create a sample booklet for students to refer to as they work on their projects.

Introducing the Project

1. Tell students that they will be creating booklets to summarize what they've learned about summaries. Display the sample booklet you made. Keep it available for students to study.

2. Distribute and discuss directions for the project on the Student Project Sheets. Make sure everyone understands how to do the project. (NOTE: For the summaries based on the reproducibles, students can use notebook paper.)

3. As you model the construction of a booklet, have students complete the steps with you. Align the five sheets of construction paper, and then fold them in half to create a 10-page booklet that measures 9 inches by 12 inches. Staple the pages together along the fold. (You may also staple together 10 smaller sheets of construction paper along one of the long edges.)

Idea

I like to pass out pocket folders to my students so that they can keep all the materials for this project organized in one place.

Objective

Students use a variety of graphic organizers to write a summary of a book.

Materials

5 sheets of 12- by 18-inch construction paper for each student, notebook paper, markers, stapler, glue, calendar chart, sample booklet, list of books (optional)

Reproducibles

(Make 1 copy for each student.):

Student Project Sheet, pages 57–58

Who? Character Summary, page 59

What? Events Summary, page 60

Where and When? Setting Summary, page 61

Why and How? Reflection, page 62

Summarizing a Favorite Book Rubric, page 63

MANIAC MAGEE
BY: Jerry Spinelli

SUMMARIZING FINAL PROJECT

By: Mimi L.
June 9

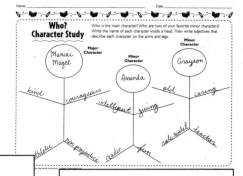

Name _____   Date _____

Who?
Character Study

Who is the main character? Who are two of your favorite minor characters? Write the name of each character inside a head. Then write adjectives that describe each character on the arms and legs.

Major Character — Maniac Magee
kind, courageous, intelligent, athletic, non-prejudice

Minor Character — Amanda
giving, reader, fun, role model, teacher

Minor Character — Grayson
old, caring

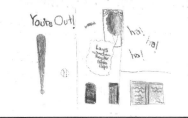

CHARACTER SUMMARY PARAGRAPH

"Maniac, Maniac he's so cool, don't go to school, runs all night, runs all right, kissed a bull."

Maniac was a 10 year old legend. Maniac wasn't his really name, but when his parents died, his life and name changed too (Jeffrey Magee). He was known for how fast he could run, how high he could jump, and how he could get any knot untied. He is best known for his courage in uniting white West End and black East End. The rest is history!

You're Out!   ha! ha! ha!

THE BIG SUMMARY

"Maniac, Maniac he's so cool, don't go to school, runs all night, runs all right, kissed a bull." Maniac Magee is the star of the book. He united 2 ends of a town, Two Mills, Pennsylvania, in a very unique way because he did not see their color differences. They say he was color blind while the whole town saw very distinctively the colors of black and white and discriminated against the color they were not.

Maniac was a 10 year old legend. Maniac wasn't his really name, but when his parents died, his life and name changed too (Jeffrey Magee). He was known for how fast he could run, how high he could jump, and how he could get any knot untied. He is best known for his courage in uniting white West End and black East End. The rest is history!

Two Mills, Pennsylvania seems to be a divided city. There is a West End that has white citizens and the East End has black citizens. Maniac liked the West End because he liked to visit Cobble's Corner where he untied the largest knot and became a legend there. He also met Grayson there at the Elmwood Park Zoo. Maniac liked the East End because Amanda Beale, a young blank girl, let him borrow a book and then a beautiful friendship between the two ignited. Her family allowed Maniac to live there. They really treated him like part of the family.

Because Maniac Magee did not have a place to live, he roamed around the town sometimes making peace and sometimes a little trouble. He intervened at a baseball game and showed McNab that he was not afraid of him. He actually hit several home-runs, and McNab started to respect Maniac. Then, he asked him to live with him. What an experience this was! The McNab family had snakes that lived in their home, and very little parent supervision. The boys within the family played with weapons and used foul language, but it was this experience with this family that helped Maniac join the two sides of the town together.

Assessing the Project

❀ **Presentation:** Invite students to share the summaries of their books with the class. Let them choose which part of their booklets they would like to present (or have presented) to show their process. Encourage a question-and-answer period. When students show interest in the book being summarized, point out that writing effective summaries is the job of a book reviewer—a good summary will entice other readers to read the book.

❀ **Assessment:** Use the rubric on page 63 to grade the projects. Attach a rubric to the back of each student's booklet.

Summarizing A Favorite Book
Student Project Sheet

Cover Page
Write the book title and author, your name, and the date. Also write the project title: Summarizing Final Project

Table of Contents
Complete this page last. Don't forget to number pages 1–9!

Page 1: Who? Summary
Complete the reproducible with details about the main character and two minor characters. Then glue it to this page in your booklet.

Page 2: Character Summary
Now write a summary paragraph about the main character and his or her role in the story. Glue it to this page.

Page 3: What? Summary
Complete the reproducible by writing down the most serious problems the character faces and his or her solutions. Then list five main events in the book. Glue it to this page.

MANIAC MAGEE
BY: Jerry Spinelli

SUMMARIZING FINAL PROJECT

By: Mimi L.
June 9

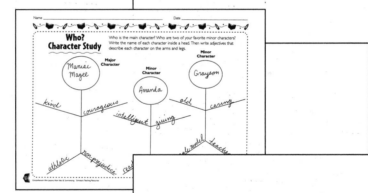

Who? Character Study
Who is the main character? Who are two of your favorite minor characters? Write the name of each character inside a head. Then write adjectives that describe each character on the arms and legs.

Major Character: Maniac Magee — kind, courageous, intelligent, athletic, non-prejudice
Minor Character: Amanda — giving
Minor Character: Grayson — old, caring

CHARACTER SUMMARY PARAGRAPH

"Maniac, Maniac he's so cool, don't go to school, runs all night, runs all right, kissed a bull."

Maniac was a 10 year old legend. Maniac wasn't his really name, but when his parents died, his life and name changed too (Jeffrey Magee). He was known for how fast he could run, how high he could jump, and how he could get any knot untied. He is best known for his courage in uniting white West End and black East End. The rest is history!

What? Events Study
Identify the problems the main character faces. How does he or she solve them? Describe five main events in the story.

Problems
Maniac intervenes at a baseball game & shows McNab that he's not afraid of him- he hits several home runs.
Maniac didn't have a place to stay

Solutions
McNab starts to respect Maniac & is nicer to him. He even allows him to live with him awhile.
Amanda Beale's family invites him in.

Main Events
1. Amanda allowed Maniac to borrow a book.
2. Maniac met McNab - the cool kid on the West End.
3. Maniac unties worst knot at Cobble's Corner.
4. Maniac meets Grayson at the Zoo.
5. Maniac unites West End & East End.

Page 4: Events Summary

Write a summary of the problems and solutions and the main events. Glue it to this page.

Page 5: Where and When? Summary

Complete the reproducible to describe the settings. Glue it to this page.

Page 6: Setting Summary

Summarize how the setting played a role in the story. Spend the most time on the main setting. Glue it to this page.

Page 7: Why and How? Summary

Complete the reproducible and glue it to this page.

Page 8: Reflection Summary

Why do you think the author wrote the story?

How did the story relate to your own life?

Write a paragraph and then glue it to this page.

Page 9: The Big Summary

Combine all your summaries into one big summary. Include an introductory paragraph.

MAJOR EVENT SUMMARY

Because Maniac Magee did not have a place to live, he roamed around the town sometimes making peace and sometimes a little trouble. He intervened at a baseball game and showed McNab that he was not afraid of him. He actually hit several home-runs, and McNab started to respect Maniac. Then, he asked him to live with him. What an experience this was! The McNab family had snakes that lived in their home, and very little parent supervision. The boys within the family played with weapons and used foul language, but it was this experience with this family that helped Maniac join the two sides of the town together.

Maniac wandered onto the East End of town and met Amanda Beale who allowed Maniac to borrow a book. This friendship gave Maniac another home for awhile. He loved Amanda's family. It was very unique on the East End for an African-American family to take in a little, white boy, but in the end, it was this event that helped Maniac join th...

Eventually, Maniac unites the West and East en... Beale's, to help him out.

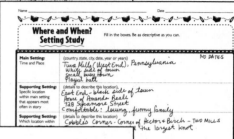

Where and When? Setting Study Fill in the boxes. Be as descriptive as you can.

NO DATES

Main Setting: Time and Place	(country, state, city, date, year or years) Two Mills (West End), Pennsylvania White side of town Small busy town Played ball
Supporting Setting: Specific location within main setting that appears most often in story	(details to describe this location) East End - black side of town Home of Amanda Beale 728 Sycamore Street Comfortable! loving, funny family
Supporting Setting: Which location within	(details to describe this location) Cobble's Corner - Corner of Hector & Birch - Two Mills the largest knot

---

SETTING SUMMARY

Two Mills, Pennsylvania seems to be a divided city. There is a West End that has white citizens and the East End has black citizens.

Maniac liked the West End because he liked to visit Cobble's Corner where he untied the largest knot and became a legend there. He also met Grayson there at the Elmwood Park Zoo.

Maniac liked the East End because Amanda Beale, a young blank girl, let him borrow a book and then a beautiful friendship between the two ignited. Her family allowed Maniac to live there. They really treated him like part of the family.

Maniac liked Two Mills better after he united the 2 sides and this my friends, is a whole nother story.

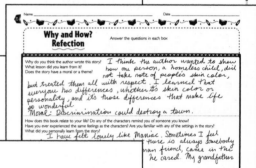

Why and How? Reflection Answer the questions in each box

Why do you think the author wrote this story! What lesson did you learn from it? Does the story have a moral or a theme?

I think the author wanted to show how one person, a homeless child, did not take note of people's skin color, but treated them all with respect. I learned that everyone has differences, whether it's skin color or personality, and it's those differences that make life so wonderful.
Moral: Discrimination could destroy a town.

How does this story relate to your life! Do any of the characters remind you of someone you know! Have you ever experienced the same feelings as the characters! Are you familiar with any of the settings in the story? What did you personally learn from the story!

I have felt lonely like Maniac. Sometimes I feel there is always somebody ...an friend, came in the ...he cared. My grandfather

---

REFLECTION SUMMARY

This story means a lot to me because I have felt lonely just like Maniac did. Just when I thought nobody cared about how I felt about losing the basketball game for our team, my grandfather came over and told me his sports failures.

Grayson showed up to cheer up Maniac in the knick of time. Maniac seemed to be dying in the buffalo stables at the zoo from having little food, but Grayson took him to his home, YMCA, and cleaned him, bathed him, and fed him the most wonderful food. They became very close friends and shared all events together. Neither one of them were lonely anymore.

This story also means a lot to me because recently, I stopped a grou... of the slower learning kids. I was proud of myself from stopping a g... discriminating against this student. Maniac showed both ends of the... differences, but it should enhance life rather than split life. He did... showed a town how to stop discriminating against each other.

THE BIG SUMMARY

"Maniac, Maniac he's so cool, don't go to school, runs all night, runs all right, kissed a bull." Maniac Magee is the star of the book. He united 2 ends of a town, Two Mills, Pennsylvania, in a very unique way because he did not see their color differences. They say he was color blind while the whole town saw very distinctively the colors of black and white and discriminated against the color they were not.

Maniac was a 10 year old legend. Maniac wasn't his really name, but when his parents died, his life and name changed too (Jeffrey Magee). He was known for how fast he could run, how high he could jump, and how he could get any knot untied. He is best known for his courage in uniting white West End and black East End. The rest is history!

Two Mills, Pennsylvania seems to be a divided city. There is a West End that has white citizens and the East End has black citizens. Maniac liked the West End because he liked to visit Cobble's Corner where he untied the largest knot and became a legend there. He also met Grayson there at the Elmwood Park Zoo. Maniac liked the East End because Amanda Beale, a young blank girl, let him borrow a book and then a beautiful friendship between the two ignited. Her family allowed Maniac to live there. They really treated him like part of the family.

Because Maniac Magee did not have a place to live, he roamed around the town sometimes making peace and sometimes a little trouble. He intervened at a baseball game and showed McNab that he was not afraid of him. He actually hit several home-runs, and McNab started to respect Maniac. Then, he asked him to live with him. What an experience this was! The McNab family had snakes that lived in their home, and very little parent supervision. The boys within the family played with weapons and used foul language, but it was this experience with this family that helped Maniac join the two sides of the town together.

Comprehension Mini-Lessons: Main Idea & Summarizing   Scholastic Teaching Resources

Name _____

Date _____

Who?
Character Summary

Who is the main character? Who are two of your favorite minor characters? Write the name of each character inside a head. Then write adjectives that describe each character on the arms and legs.

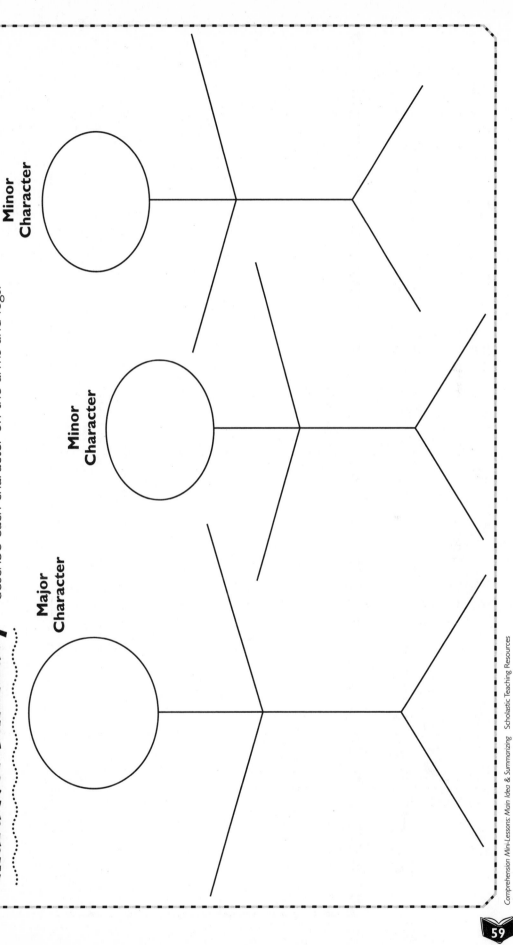

Major Character

Minor Character

Minor Character

Name _____

Date _____

What?
Events Summary

Identify the problems the main character faces. How does he or she solve them? Describe five main events in the story.

Problems

Solutions

Main Events

1. _____

2. _____

3. _____

4. _____

5. _____

Comprehension Mini-Lessons: Main Idea & Summarizing Scholastic Teaching Resources

Where and When?
Setting Summary

Fill in the boxes. Be as descriptive as you can.

Main Setting: Time and Place	(country, state, city, date, year or years)
Supporting Setting: Which location within the main setting appears most often in the story?	(details to describe this location)
Supporting Setting: Which location within the main setting is the next most important?	(details to describe this location)
Supporting Setting: Which location within the main setting is the next most important?	(details to describe this location)

Why and How? Reflection

Answer the questions in each box.

Why do you think the author wrote this story?
What lesson did you learn from it?
Does the story have a moral or a theme?

How does this book relate to your life? Do any of the characters remind you of someone you know?
Have you ever experienced the same feelings as the characters? Are you familiar with any of the settings in the story?
What did you personally learn from the story?

Summarizing a Favorite Book Rubric

Student's Name _____ Date _____

CRITERIA	Incomplete 0	Okay 1	Good 2	Outstanding 3

Assignment

1. Cover and table of contents: The cover has your name, title and author of the featured book, date, and title of the booklet. The table of contents lists all pages in the booklet with titles and corresponding page numbers.

2. Page 2: The Who? Character Summary reproducible is completed and attached.

3. Page 3: It has summary about the main character and his/her role in the story.

4. Page 4: The What? Major Events Summary reproducible is completed and attached.

5. Page 5: It has summary of the major problems the main character faces and their solutions.

6. Page 6: The Where and When? Setting Summary reproducible is completed and attached.

7. Page 7: It has summary of the different settings and their role in the story.

8. Page 8: The Why and How? Reflection Summary reproducible is completed and attached.

9. Page 9: It answers these questions: Why do you think the author wrote this story? How does this story relate to your life?

10. Page 10: It has a big summary that combines all the summaries. It also has introductory and concluding paragraphs.

11. Overall understanding of summarization

Style and Structure
12. Spelling, punctuation, capitalization, and grammar have been checked.

Presentation
13. Neatness

What you did well:

Opportunities for growth:

TOTAL SCORE: ____/39

Teacher Resources

Beech, Linda Ward. *Ready-to-Go Reproducibles: Short Reading Passages and Graphic Organizers to Build Comprehension (Grades 4–5 and Grades 6–8).* New York: Scholastic Inc., 2001.

Billmeyer, Rachel and Mary Lee Barton. *Teaching Reading in the Content Areas: If Not Me, Then Who?* Aurora, CO: McREL, 1998.

Bixby, M. *Prove It: Whole Language Strategies for Secondary Students.* Katonah, NY: Richard Owen Publishing Co., 1988.

Howard, Mary. *Helping Your Struggling Students Be More Successful Readers (Grades 4–6).* Tulsa, OK: Reading Connections, Inc., 2003.*

Robb, Laura. *Reading Strategies That Work.* New York: Scholastic Inc., 1995.

Wilhelm, Jeffrey D. *Action Strategies for Deepening Comprehension.* New York: Scholastic Inc., 2002.

Wilhelm, Jeffrey D. *Improving Comprehension With Think-Aloud Strategies.* New York: Scholastic Inc., 2001.

* This book is available at *http://www.drmaryhoward.com.*